THE WAY
OF
PRAYER

POPE JOHN PAUL II

THE WAY
OF
PRAYER

CROSSROAD · NEW YORK

1995

The Crossroad Publishing Company
370 Lexington Avenue, New York, NY 10017

Copyright © by Tony Castle, 1981, 1995

Excerpted from *Through the Year with Pope John Paul II* and *Daily Readings with Pope John Paul II*, edited and compiled by Tony Castle and published by Hodder & Stoughton.

Illustrations from *Clip Art of the Old Testament* and *Clip Art: Block Prints for Sundays*, both by Helen Siegl. Reproduced with permission of The Liturgical Press.

Printed in the United States of America

Library of Congress Cataloging-in-Publication Data

John Paul II, Pope, 1920–
    The way of prayer / Pope John Paul II; edited and compiled by Tony Castle.
        p.   cm.
    ISBN 0-8245-2008-4
    1. Prayer—Catholic Church—Meditation.   2. Catholic Church—Meditations.   I. Castle, Tony.   II. Title.
BV215.J56   1995
248.3'2—dc20
                                                95-30096
                                                CIP

WHY DO I PRAY?

*If there is anything you need,
pray for it asking God for it with
prayer and thanksgiving.*

— PHIL. 4:6

Why do I pray? Why do you pray? Why do people pray? Why do Christians, Muslims, Buddhists, pagans pray? Why do people pray, even those who think that they do not pray?

The answer is very simple: *I pray because God exists*. I know that God exists, therefore I pray. Some people answer boldly: "I know that God exists." Some people have rather a different answer to the question: "Why do you pray?" Maybe they do not say with such certainty: "I know." Maybe they say rather, "I believe." Maybe the answer is even: "I am seeking."

HOW DO I PRAY?

Pray constantly, and for all things give thanks to God.

— 1 THESS. 5:17

There are several definitions of prayer. But it is most often called a talk, or a conversation, with God. When we hold a conversation with someone, we not only speak, but we also listen. *Prayer, therefore, is also listening.*

It consists of listening to hear the interior voice of grace. Listening to hear the call. And then, as you ask me how the Pope prays, I answer you: like every Christian: he speaks and he listens. Sometimes, he prays without words, and then he listens all the more. The most important thing is precisely what he "hears." And he also tries to unite prayer with his obligations, his activities, his work, and *to unite his work with prayer.*

In this way, day after day, he tries to carry out his "service," his "ministry," which comes to him from the will of Christ and from the living tradition of the Church.

THE NEED FOR PRAYER

Lord, teach us to pray.

— LUKE 11:1

When, on the slopes of the Mount of Olives, the Apostles addressed Jesus with these words they were not asking an ordinary question, but with spontaneous trust, they were expressing one of the deepest needs of the human heart.

To tell the truth, *today's world does not make much room for that need.* The hectic pace of daily activity, combined with the noisy and often frivo-

lous invasiveness of the means of com-
munication, is certainly not something
conducive to the interior recollection
required for prayer.

In Christian circles, too, there is a widespread "functional" view of prayer that threatens to compromise its transcendent nature. Some claim that one truly finds God by being open to one's neighbor. Therefore, prayer would not mean being removed from the world's distractions in order to be recollected in conversation with God; it would rather be expressed in an unconditional commitment to charity for others. Authentic prayer, therefore, would be the works of charity, and they alone.

In reality, because they are creatures and of themselves incomplete and needy, human beings spontaneously turn to him who is the Source of every gift, in order to praise him, make intercession, and in him seek to fulfil the tormenting desire that enflames their hearts. St. Augustine understood this quite well when he noted: "You have made us for yourself, O Lord, and our hearts are restless until they rest in you" (*Confessions*, I.1).

For this very reason the experience of prayer, as a basic act of the believer, is common to all religions, including those in which there is only a rather vague belief in a personal God or in which it is confused by false representations.

Prayer particularly belongs to the Christian religion, in which it occupies a central position. Jesus urges us to "pray always without becoming weary" (Luke 18:1). Christians know

THE DIFFERENT DIMENSIONS OF PRAYER

When he had finished talk-ing to Abraham the Lord God went away, and Abraham returned home.

— GEN. 18:33

Prayer is a conversation. We know quite well that it is possible to hold all sorts of conversations. Sometimes conversation is simply an exchange of words: we remain, as it were, on the surface.

But our conversations are truly profound when we do not simply exchange words, when we do not simply toss words about, but when we exchange thoughts. Our conversations are truly profound when we exchange our hearts, our feelings, when we exchange in some measure our own "I."

People's prayers, *too, have very different dimensions, very different depths.* Not just different outward forms. When Muslims pray, for example, they pray with such great courage, everywhere at the appointed times calling upon their Allah. When Buddhists pray, they enter into complete concentration, as if to lose themselves completely in this concentration.

When Christians pray, they take from Christ the word "Father," which through the Spirit covers everything their spirit needs.

THE IMPORTANCE OF PRAYER

Ask, and it will be given to you; search, and you will find; knock, and the door will be opened to you.

— LUKE 11:9

A model of such persevering prayer, humble and, at the same time, confident, is found in the Old Testament in Abraham, who beseeches God for the salvation of Sodom and Gomorrah, if there were at least ten righteous men to be found there.

In this way, therefore, *we must encourage ourselves more and more to prayer.* We must often remember the exhortation of Christ: "Ask, and it will be given to you." In particular, we must remember it when we lose confidence or the desire to pray.

We must also learn anew to pray, always. It often happens that we dispense ourselves from praying with the excuse that we are unable to do so. If we really do not know how to pray, then it is all the more necessary to learn. That is important for everyone, and it seems to be particularly important for the young, who often neglect the prayer they learned as children, because it seems to them too childish, naive, and superficial.

Such a state of mind is, on the contrary, an indirect incentive to deepen one's prayer, to make it more thoughtful, more mature, *to seek support for it in the Word of God himself and in the Holy Spirit,* who "expresses our plea in a way that could never be put into words" (Rom. 8:26).

THE MEANING
OF PRAYER

*Abraham replied, "I am bold
indeed to speak like this to my
Lord, I who am dust and ashes."*

— GEN. 18:27

What does praying mean? *Praying
means feeling one's own insufficiency,*
feeling one's own insufficiency through
the various necessities that human beings have to face, necessities that are
part of our lives — such as, for example, the need for bread to which Christ
refers in the example of that man who

wakes up his friend at midnight to ask him for bread.

Similar necessities are numerous. The need for bread is, in a way, a symbol of all material necessities, the necessities of the human body, the necessities of this existence that springs from the fact that the human being is a body. But the range of these necessities is wider.

To the answers of Christ, there also pertains the marvelous event in Genesis, of which Abraham is the main character. And the main problem is that of Sodom and Gomorrah; or in other words, that of good and evil, of sin and guilt; namely, it is the problem of justice and mercy. This conversation between Abraham and God is splendid and proves that praying means moving continually in the sphere of justice and mercy; between justice and mercy, it is penetrating into God himself.

Praying means being aware, being completely aware, of all human necessities, of the whole truth about the human being. And it means in light of this truth, whose direct subject is I myself — and not only I but also my neighbor, all people, the whole of humankind — and in light of this truth, addressing God as Father.

LEARNING THE FATHER

What father among you would hand his son a stone when he asked for bread?

— LUKE 11:11

According to Christ's answer to the request, "Teach us to pray," everything is reduced to this single concept: *to learn to pray means "to learn the Father."* If we learn the Father reality in the full sense of the word, in its full dimension, we have learned everything.

To learn the Father means finding the answer to the question about how

— 23 —

to pray, because to pray also means finding the answer to a series of questions that, for example, arise from the fact that I pray and in some cases my prayer is not granted.

Christ gives indirect answers to these questions as well. He gives them in the whole Gospel and in the whole of Christian experience. *To learn who the Father is means learning what absolute trust is.*

To learn the Father means acquiring the certainty that he absolutely cannot refuse anything. He does not refuse you even when everything, materially and psychologically, seems to indicate refusal. He never refuses you.

OUR PRAYER ALWAYS ANSWERED

How much more will the heavenly Father give the Holy Spirit to those who ask him!

— LUKE 11:13

Learning to pray means "learning the Father" in this way: learning to be sure that the Father never refuses you anything, but that on the contrary, he gives the Holy Spirit to those who ask him.

The gifts we ask for are various; they are our necessities. *We ask ac-*

cording to our needs and it cannot be otherwise. Christ confirms this attitude of ours: yes, it is so: you must ask according to your needs, as you feel them. As these necessities shake you, often painfully, so you must pray.

On the other hand, when it is a question of the answer to every request of yours it is always given through a substantial gift: *the Father gives us the Holy Spirit.* And he does so in consideration of his Son.

For this reason he gave his Son, gave his Son for the sins of the world; he gave his Son facing all the needs of the world, all the needs of humanity, so as to be able always to give the Holy Spirit in this crucified and risen Son. This is his gift.

THE GIFT OF THE FATHER

On the day I called, you answered me, O Lord.

— Ps. 138:3

Learning to pray means learning the Father and learning absolute trust in him who always offers us this greatest gift. And in offering it he never deceives us. If sometimes, or even often, we do not directly receive what we ask for, *in this great gift — when it is offered to us — all other gifts are contained,* even if we do not always realize this.

The example that struck me most in the past is that of a man whom I met in a hospital. He was seriously ill as a result of wounds suffered during the Warsaw Insurrection. In that hospital he spoke to me of his extraordinary happiness.

This man achieved happiness by some other way because visibly, judging his physical state from the medical point of view, there was no reason to be so happy, to feel so well, and to consider himself heard by God. Yet he was heard in another aspect of his humanity. He recalled the gift in which he found his happiness despite so much unhappiness.

THE "OUR FATHER"

Pray then in this way: "Our Father in Heaven...."

— MATT. 6:9

When the disciples asked the Lord Jesus: "Teach us to pray," he replied with the words of the prayer "Our Father," thus creating a model that is concrete and at the same time universal.

In fact, all that can and must be said to the Father is contained in those seven requests, which we all know by

heart. There is such a simplicity in
them that even a child can learn them,
and also such a depth that a whole life
can be spent meditating on the mean-
ing of each of them. Is this not so?
Does not each of them speak to us, one
after the other, of what is essential of
our existence, directed completely to
God, to the Father? Does it not speak
to us of our "daily bread," of "for-
giveness of our trespasses as we also
forgive them," and at the same time of
"preservation from temptation" and
"deliverance from evil"?

When, in answer to the request
of the disciples, "Teach us to pray,"
Christ utters the words of his prayer,
he teaches not only the words, but he
teaches that in our talk with the Father

there must be complete sincerity and full openness.

ALL-EMBRACING PRAYER

Through him, let us offer God an unending sacrifice of praise.

— HEB. 13:15

Prayer must embrace everything that is part of our lives. It cannot be something additional or marginal to our lives. *Everything must find in it its true voice* — even things that burden us, things of which we are ashamed, things that by their very nature separate us from God. This above all: it is prayer that always, first of all and essentially, demolishes the barrier that sin and evil may have raised between us and God.

Through prayer the whole world must find its proper direction, that is, an orientation toward God: my interior world and also the objective world, the world in which we live and the world of our experience.

If we are converted to God, everything in us is directed to him. Prayer is the expression of this being directed to God, and it is, at the same time, the source of our continual conversion.

Prayer is the way of the Word that

embraces everything. It is the way of the eternal Word that goes to the depths of so many hearts, that brings back to the Father everything that has its origin in him.

Prayer is the sacrifice of our lips. It is, as St. Ignatius of Antioch writes, spring water that murmurs within us and says: "Come to the Father."

ALL PRAYER IS OUTGOING

Pray for one another, and this will cure you; the heartfelt prayer of a good man works very powerfully.
— JAMES 5:16

Prayer has a social significance. Let us never think that those who devote a great deal of time to prayer serve only themselves and their own inner longings. They also serve the Church, the community, society, because that is the sense of their prayer; they share themselves with others.

Let us remember that prayer shares

itself with others. It never remains in isolation; it always penetrates the walls of the soul and reaches others.

PRAYER GROUPS

God gives power and strength to his people.

— Ps. 68:35

Today there are many communities that pray, pray as perhaps they have never done before, in a different way, a more complete and richer way, *with a greater receptiveness for that gift that the Father gives us.* They also pray

with a new human expression of this receptiveness and I should say with a new cultural program of new prayer. Such communities are numerous. I wish to unite with them wherever they may be: all over the earth.

This great revolution of prayer is the fruit of the gift, and it is also the testimony of the vast needs of people today and of the threats looming over us and over the modern world.

I think that Abraham's prayer and its content is very relevant in the times in which we live. Such a prayer is so necessary, to negotiate with God for every just person, to redeem the world from injustice. *A prayer that makes its way into God's heart,* so to speak, between what is justice and what is mercy in it, is indispensable.

PRAYER IN SECRET

*When you pray, go to your private
room and, when you have shut
your door, pray to your Father.*

When he says, "Go to your room and
shut your door," he is talking about
an ascetic effort of the human spirit
that must not be confined within oneself. *This shutting-in of oneself is, at
the same time, the deepest opening of
the human heart.*

It is indispensable for the purpose of
meeting the Father and must be under-

taken for this purpose. "Your Father who sees in secret will reward you."

Here it is a question of acquiring again the simplicity of thought, of will, and of heart that is indispensable if one is to meet God in one's own "self." And God is waiting for this, in order to approach human beings who are absorbed interiorly and at the same time open to his word and his love!

God wishes to communicate himself to the soul thus disposed. He wishes to give it truth and love, which have their real source in him.

THE HOLY SPIRIT PRAYING IN US

When we cannot choose words in order to pray properly, the Spirit himself expresses our plea.

— ROM. 8:26

Prayer is indispensable for persevering in pursuit of the good, indispensable for overcoming the trials life brings to human beings owing to human weakness. *Prayer is a strength for the weak and weakness for the strong!* This is what the Apostle is saying, "the Spirit expresses our plea in a way that could never be put into words" (Rom. 8:26).

Prayer can be said to be a constitutive element of human existence in the world. Human existence is "being directed toward God." At the same time it is "being within the dimensions of God," a humble but courageous entering into the depths of God's thought, the depths of his mystery and his plans. It is a kind of drawing on the source of divine power: will and grace.

It is also, as St. Paul says, the work of the Holy Spirit in us. And the Spirit, says the Apostle in another letter, "reaches the depths of everything, even the depths of God" (1 Cor. 2:10).

PRAYER AND GOOD WORKS

If good works do not go with faith, it is quite dead.

— JAMES 2:17

In prayer we come to understand the Beatitudes and the reasons why we must live them. Only through prayer can we begin to see all the aspirations of humanity from the perspective of Christ. Without the intuitions of prayer we would never grasp all the dimensions of human development and the urgency for the Christian community to commit itself to this work.

Prayer calls us to examine our consciences on all the issues that affect humanity. It calls us to ponder our personal and collective responsibility before the judgment of God and in the light of human solidarity. Hence *prayer is able to transform the world.*

Everything is new with prayer, both for individuals and communities. New goals and new ideals emerge. Christian dignity and action are reaffirmed. The commitments of our baptism, confirmation, and Holy Orders take on new urgency. The horizons of conjugal love and of the mission of the family are vastly extended in prayer.

THE CALL TO PERFECTION

Master, what good deed must I do to possess eternal life?

— MATT. 19:16

In the Gospel story we see that the rich young man, having affirmed that he has kept the commandments, adds: "What more do I need to do?" (Matt. 19:20). That young heart, moved by God's grace, felt a desire for greater generosity, more commitment, greater love. This desire for more is characteristic of youth; a heart that is in love does not calculate, does not begrudge;

it wants to give of itself without measure.

"Jesus, looking at him, loved him and said to him, 'You are lacking in one thing. Go, sell what you have, and give to the poor and you will have treasure in heaven; then come, follow me' " (Mark 10:21).

To those who entered the path of life by observing the commandments, by observing the law of love like that young man (cf. Luke 18:21), the Lord proposes new horizons; *the Lord proposes to them means that are loftier and calls them to commit themselves to this love without reserve. To discover this call, this vocation, is to realize that Christ is looking on you and inviting you by his glance to give yourself totally in love.* Before this glance, before his love, the heart opens its doors gradually and is capable of saying "Yes."

BE GENEROUS!

When the young man heard these words he went away sad.

— MATT. 19:22

Be generous in giving to your brothers and sisters; be generous in sacrificing for others and in work; be generous in the fulfillment of your family and civic obligations; *be generous in*

building the civilization of love. Above all, if some of you hear the call to follow Christ more closely, to dedicate your entire heart to him, like the Apostles John and Paul, be generous, do not be afraid, because you have nothing to fear when the prize that you await is God himself, for whom, sometimes without ever knowing it, all young people are searching.

The last part of this story states: "When the young man heard this statement, he went away sad, for he had many possessions."

"The young man...went away sad." St. Matthew relates what is in reality the personal experience of many — who knows how many of you? — *the sadness that one feels when one says "No" to God,* when one does not keep the commandments or does not want to answer his call.

THE SECRET OF HAPPINESS

*He went away sad, because he
was a man of great wealth.*

— MATT. 19:22

That young man "had many possessions." He had, most of all, youth to
offer: an entire life that he could commit to the Lord. What happiness if he
had only said "Yes"! What wonders
God could have done in a generous
person who offered himself without
reserve. But no, he preferred "his
goods": his peace, his house, his plans,
his selfishness. *Faced with choosing be-*

*tween God and self, he preferred the
latter, and he went away sad,* as the
Gospel tells us. He opted for his own
selfishness and found sadness. Whenever in your following of Christ you
are faced with choice between him,
between one of his commandments,
and the passing pleasure of something material and tangible, whenever
you are faced with choosing between
helping someone in need and your
own interest, *when, in the final analysis, you have to choose between love
and egoism, remember the example
of Christ and valiantly choose love.*
Young people who are listening to me,
young people who, more than anything else, want to know what you
must do to gain eternal life: always say

"Yes" to God and he will fill you with his happiness.

DECISIONS REQUIRE PRAYER

Jesus spent the whole night in prayer to God.... He summoned his disciples and picked out twelve of them.

— LUKE 6:12

Christian sensitivity is dependent on prayer. Prayer is an essential condition — even if not the only one —

for a correct reading of the "signs of the times." Without prayer deception is inevitable in a matter of such importance.

Decisions require prayer; decisions of magnitude require sustained prayer.

Jesus himself gives us the example. Before calling his disciples and selecting the twelve, Jesus passed the night, on the mountain, in communion with his Father. For Jesus, prayer to his Father meant not only light and strength. It also meant confidence, trust, and joy. His human nature exulted in the joy that came to him in prayer. *The measure of the Church's joy in any age is in proportion to her prayer.*

The gauge of her strength and the condition for her confidence are fidelity to prayer. The mysteries of Christ are disclosed to those who approach him in prayer. The full application of the Second Vatican Council will forever be conditioned by perseverance in prayer. The great strides made by the laity of the Church in realizing how much they belong to the Church — how much they are the Church — can be explained in the last analysis only by grace and its acceptance in prayer.

SCRIPTURE GENERATES PRAYER

Faith comes from what is preached, and what is preached comes from the word of Christ.

— ROM. 10:17

In the life of the Church today we frequently perceive that the gift of prayer is linked to the word of God. A renewal in discovering the Sacred Scriptures has brought forth the fruits of prayer. God's word, embraced and meditated on, has the power to bring human hearts into ever greater communion with the Most Holy Trinity. Over and over again this has taken place in the Church in our day. The benefits received through prayer linked to the word of God call forth in all of us a further response of prayer — the prayer of praise and thanksgiving.

The word of God generates prayer in the whole community. At the same time it is in prayer that the word of God is understood, applied, and lived. For all of us who are ministers of the Gospel, with the pastoral responsibil-

ity of announcing the message in season and out of season and of scrutinizing the reality of daily life in the light of God's holy word, prayer is the context in which we prepare the proclamation of faith. *All evangelization is prepared in prayer*; in prayer it is first applied to ourselves; in prayer it is then offered to the world.

PRAYER IS POSSIBLE

Jesus told them a parable about the need to pray continually and never lose heart.

— LUKE 18:1

We often say that we don't know how to pray. How to pray? This is a simple matter. I would say: *Pray any way you like, so long as you do pray.* Say prayers that your mother taught you. Pray any way you like, but you must pray.

And never say: "I don't pray because I don't know how to pray!" Because this simply isn't true. Everyone knows how to pray. The words of prayer are simple and the rest follows.

To say: "I don't know how to pray" means that you are deceiving yourself. Yourself and who else? Who can you deceive about this? It always means some smallness of heart. Some lack of good will. Or sometimes of courage. It is possible to pray, and necessary to pray.

Pray any way you like. From a book or from memory, it's all the same. Maybe just in thought. We can pray perfectly when, for example, we are

out in the mountains or on a lake and we feel at one with nature. Nature speaks for us or rather speaks to us. We pray perfectly.

LISTENING TO CHRIST

This is my Son, the Beloved; he enjoys my favor. Listen to him.

— MATT. 17:5

What does it mean, to listen to Christ?

The whole Church must always give an answer to this question in the dimensions of the generations, periods, and changing social, economic, and political conditions. The answer must be true, it must be sincere — just as the teaching of Christ, his Gospel, and then Gethsemane, the Cross, and the Resurrection are true and sincere.

Each of us must always give an answer to this question: whether our Christianity, our life, are in conformity with faith, if they are true and sincere.

The answer will be a little different every time: the answer of the father and mother of a family will be different, that of engaged couples different, that of the child will be different, and that of the boy and the girl will be different, that of the old person will be different, and that of the sick person confined to a bed of pain will be different, that of the person of science, of politics, of culture, of economy will be different, that of the person who does hard physical work will be different, that of the Religious Sister or Brother will be different, that of the priest, of